Homosexuality in the Bible

Verse-by-Verse Exposition of the "Gay Verses"

Dr. E.B.

Contents

Preface

There are allegedly six direct references to homosexuality in the bible, with three in the Old Testament and three in the New Testament. In this concise book, my focus is specifically on these biblical verses pertaining to homosexuality, deliberately not addressing other aspects of the LGBTQ+ spectrum, like transgender issues. This decision stems from my belief that topics such as transgenderism necessitate a more expansive dialogue, one that transcends solely theological debate. Additionally, the Bible's references are primarily focused on homosexuality.

I am not gay, nor do I have any gay family members or very close friends who are gay, and therefore do not have a horse in this race. My interest in this subject arises from a deep-seated desire to uncover the truth independent of prevailing opinions. Despite my conservative upbringing, I have recognized that some of my conservative views were more tradition-based than rooted in objective truth, like with the case of many other Christian doctrines.

My academic journey in biblical and theological studies has been a journey from ignorant and prideful confidence to humble complexity. Earning my Bachelor's degree in Bible Studies initially filled me with a sense of comprehensive understanding. However, as I progressed through my Master's in Theology and eventually completed my doctorate, I increasingly recognized the multifaceted nature of theological discourse and the complexities underlying many issues that some fundamentalist Christians perceive as straightforward.

This exploration is a reflection of my commitment to seeking truth rather than advocating for a specific agenda. While I firmly believe in the existence of God and in Jesus as Lord, I approach most theological topics with an open mind, willing to adapt and evolve my understanding based on thorough research and study. This book represents my personal investigation into the biblical texts concerning homosexuality, approached from a Christian perspective informed by my Jewish-Hebrew heritage. It is not presented as the definitive truth but rather as a summary of an individual's scholarly exploration and interpretation.

This concise "micro-book" offers an accessible, verse-by-verse exposition of the "homosexual verses" in the Bible. The book is designed to be straightforward and easy to read, providing an unbiased exploration free from the influence of preconceived religious doctrines.

Readable in just two hours, this short book is an ideal resource for anyone seeking a quick yet comprehensive understanding of these biblical passages, devoid of the traditional theological complexities often associated with conservative religious interpretations.

The author, a Jewish-Christian scholar with advanced degrees in Bible and theology, is uniquely positioned to tackle this subject. As a native Hebrew speaker and a seasoned Bible scholar, he melds his Jewish heritage with his extensive Christian education and faith. This fusion enables him to provide a guide that explores what the Bible says about homosexuality from a non-fundamentalist perspective, offering insights that are deeply rooted in the text while refreshingly liberating.

The author has decided to remain anonymous for the time being but may reveal his identity in the future if there are over a hundred positive reviews of the book on Amazon and Goodreads.

Genesis 19:1-13

"Bring them out so we may have relations with them"

[1] Now the two angels came to Sodom in the evening as Lot was sitting at the gate of Sodom. When Lot saw *them*, he stood up to meet them and bowed down *with his* face to the ground. [2] And he said, "Now behold, my lords, please turn aside into your servant's house, and spend the night, and wash your feet; then you may rise early and go on your way." They said, "No, but we shall spend the night in the public square." [3] Yet he strongly urged them, so they turned aside to him and entered his house; and he prepared a feast for them and baked unleavened bread, and they ate.

[4] Before they lay down, the men of the city—the men of Sodom—surrounded

the house, both young and old, all the people from every quarter; **5** and they called to Lot and said to him, "Where are the men [people] who came to you tonight? Bring them out to us that we may have relations with [know] them." **6** But Lot went out to them at the doorway, and shut the door behind him, **7** and said, "Please, my brothers, do not act wickedly. **8** Now look, I have two daughters who have not had relations with *any* man; please let me bring them out to you, and do to them whatever you like; only do not do anything to these men, because they have come under the shelter of my roof."

9 But they said, "Get out of the way!" They also said, "This one came in as a foreigner, and already he is acting like a judge; now we will treat you worse than them!" So they pressed hard against Lot and moved forward to break the door. **10** But the men reached out their hands and brought Lot into the house with them, and shut the door. **11** Then they struck the men who were at the doorway of the house with blindness, from the small to the great, so that they

became weary of *trying* to find the doorway.
[12] Then the *two* men said to Lot, "Whom
else do you have here? A son-in-law and
your sons and daughters, and whomever
you have in the city, bring *them* out of the
place; [13] for we are about to destroy this
place, because their outcry has become so
great before the Lord that the Lord has sent
us to destroy it."

Genesis 19:1-13

I n the Biblical narrative of Genesis 19, the imminent
destruction of Sodom is decreed due to its "great
wickedness," though the specific nature of this wickedness
is initially unarticulated. Lot, a paragon of righteousness
amidst the city's depravity, welcomes two celestial
messengers into his home, shielding them from the city's
populace who surround the house, intent on committing
a violent act against these visitors.

This incident, often taken as a condemnation of
homosexuality, prompts a critical reassessment of the
city's sin. The improbability of an exclusively homosexual
population in Sodom is starkly evident when considering
historical evidence, the psychological understanding
of sexual orientation, and the statistical average of
homosexuals in any society. Also, the narrative's assertion

that every man in Sodom, regardless of age (verse 4), participated in the action further complicates this interpretation. But more than anything, the assumption that the men of Sodom were all homosexual arises from a superficial reading of the text, neglecting the broader cultural and historical context and, most importantly, other Bible passages interpreting this infamous incident.

What Was Sodom's Great Wickedness?

As Lot and his two angelic companions traversed the city, word about Lot's extraordinary guests quickly circulated throughout Sodom. This led to a large crowd gathering at his doorstep, where they called out, "Come on, man, bring them out so we can get to know them!"

"All men"

The terms "all men," "every man," or "men of the city" often appear in the Bible, but it doesn't exclusively mean "all males." "All men" is generally understood as "everyone." For example, Psalms 116:11 states, *All men are liars.*" This doesn't imply that women always tell the truth but rather that all people, regardless of gender, are capable of lying. Similarly, in John 13:35, when Jesus tells his disciples, *"By this shall all men know that ye are my disciples, if ye have love one to another*," Jesus refers to everyone, not just men, recognizing His disciples through their love for one another.

Likewise, 1 Timothy 2:3-4 says, "*God our Saviour; Who will have all men to be saved, and to come unto the knowledge of the truth.*" Here again, "all men" means everyone, not exclusively males. This interpretation is consistent with 1 Corinthians 9:22, where Paul states, "*To the weak, I became as weak, that I might win the weak. I have become all things to all men, that I might by all means save some.*" Paul is speaking of reaching out to all people, not just males.

Consequently, it cannot be definitively stated that all the males of Sodom were present. It might be more accurate to interpret the passage as suggesting that the entire population of the city was involved. This broader interpretation could also account for the collective punishment that later ensued.

"That we may have relations [VANEDAH] with them."

The Hebrew word used in verse five is "VANEDAH," which comes from the word YADA (know) and means "that we may know." It is a term with multiple meanings depending on the context. Psalm 100:3, "Know that the

Lord Himself is God," and Isaiah 52:6, "Therefore, My people shall know My name," use that same word to speak of knowing God, unrelated to sexual activity.

However, in Genesis 4:1, where it states, *"Now Adam* **knew** *Eve his wife, and she conceived and bore Cain,"* the term "knew" is evidently used to denote a sexual act. Therefore, the interpretation remains uncertain. It is plausible to argue that "Bring them out to us that we may know them," lacking a clear and definitive connotation, was deliberately chosen to intimidate and unsettle Lot.

However, adopting a cautious approach, let's assume that Genesis 19 does indeed refer to males of all ages seeking to rape Lot's visitors. This assumption leads to a couple of important questions: Why did they express a desire to commit such an act against Lot's visitors? Why had they never threatened to rape Lot even though he had lived among them for some time?

Sexual orientation isn't the sole reason men might rape other men. In prisons, for example, heterosexual men rape other heterosexual men as a means of degradation, asserting dominance and control. It's a power play rather than a sexual act one enjoys. This behavior isn't confined to prisons; history is replete with such cases.

For instance, during the Balkan conflicts in the 1990s, there were documented cases of male-on-male rape used as a tool of war, intended to demoralize and psychologically dominate the opposing forces.

In some ancient cultures, such as in Greece and Rome, the sexual domination of one male over another could be a display of power and social hierarchy. In these societies, the act was not necessarily viewed through the lens of sexual orientation but rather as an assertion of dominance.

These and other instances demonstrate that the motivations behind such acts are complex and often rooted in social, political, and cultural contexts where power dynamics play a significant role.

Who are they asking to rape, and why?

However, exercising caution once again, let's assume that Genesis 19 does indeed refer to males seeking homosexual relations. To align this interpretation with the concept of homosexuality, Lot's visitors would need to be perceived as male humans. Yet, the text explicitly identifies them as "two angels" (verse 1). This identification raises a critical question: If, as some fundamentalist preachers claim, *"Sodom was a whole civilization of homosexuals,"*[1] then why would Lot, presumably knowledgeable about the homosexual tendencies of his city's men, even calling them "my brothers," offer his <u>female daughters</u> if he believed these men to be solely attracted to other men? Lot's decision to offer his daughters seems to contradict the notion that the men of Sodom were exclusively homosexual. Moreover, this scenario raises the possibility that the angels may have presented themselves in a form that was not overtly masculine and perhaps even feminine (as referenced in Zechariah 5:9), prompting Lot to perceive his daughters as a fitting alternative for the crowd.

What was so wicked?

Lot says to the men, "*Do not act wickedly. Now look, I have two daughters who have not had relations with any man; please let me bring them out to you, and do to them whatever you like.*" (Genesis 19:8)

Rape is a topic that is not unfamiliar in the biblical narrative, as evidenced in instances such as Genesis 34, Deuteronomy 22, and Judges 19–21. In a particularly notable episode, Lot offers his daughters to a mob to be raped to make sure they avoid wickedness. This suggests that Lot perceived the act of having sexual relations with the two angels as a greater evil than his human daughters getting raped. This distinction in Lot's judgment highlights a complex moral hierarchy in his decision-making, where he seemingly regards sexual relations with heavenly beings as a much more grievous offense than the raping of his own children.

Lot does not appear to perceive a potential rape of his daughters as "acting wickedly," at least not to the same degree as the violation of his celestial guests. This raises the question: Did Lot believe that men raping females was acceptable, but not homosexuality? This interpretation seems implausible. Clearly, both scenarios are unethical and wrong. However, Lot seems to have understood that there was something particularly "wicked" about the men of the city wanting to engage sexually with angels.

The critical factor in this scenario is the true nature of the visitors: they were angels, not human males. Engaging in sexual relations with angelic beings is an entirely different matter from homosexuality. In Lot's perception, the intent of the men of Sodom to engage sexually with these celestial entities was particularly reprehensible. This distinction underscores that their actions were not driven by homosexual desire but rather by the profound transgression of seeking to violate beings of a divine or supernatural realm.

This perspective is reinforced by Genesis 6, which implies sexual relations between angelic beings and humans:

The Nephilim were on the earth in those days, and also afterward, when the sons of God came in to the daughters of mankind, and they bore children to them. These were the mighty men who were of old, men of renown. The LORD saw how **great the wickedness** of the human race had become on the earth..."

Genesis 6:4-5

In this context, great wickedness is associated with humans having sexual relations with angelic beings. This was Sodom's wickedness as well.

The Sodom Incident in Other Bible Passages

Ezekiel 16:49-50

> Behold, this was the guilt of your sister Sodom: she and her daughters had arrogance, plenty of food, and carefree ease, but she did not help the poor and needy. So they were haughty and committed abominations before Me. Therefore I removed them when I saw *it*.

In Ezekiel 16:49-50, the reasons for the destruction of Sodom are explicitly stated, with no mention of homosexuality. Sodom's primary transgressions were characterized by a lack of compassion and social responsibility. The city faced condemnation not for homosexuality but for its arrogance, excess, and disregard for the needy. Additionally, the city was condemned for committing "abominations," which, as previously discussed, most likely referred to their desire to engage in sexual relations with angelic beings.

Ezekiel 16 challenges Fundamentalism's view of Sodom and Gomorrah's destruction as a divine indictment of homosexuality. Instead, Ezekiel presents a narrative focused on broader ethical failings—xenophobia, violence, and social injustice.

Jude 6-7 and 2 Peter 2:4-6

> And angels who did not keep their own domain but abandoned their proper dwelling place, these He has kept in eternal restraints under darkness for the judgment of the great day, just as **Sodom** and Gomorrah and the cities around them, since they **in the same way as these angels indulged in sexual perversion** and went after **strange flesh**.
>
> Jude 6-7 (bold emphasize by me)

Drawing from Jude 6-7 and 2 Peter 2:4-6, the same argument can be constructed, suggesting that the grave sin of Sodom was related to sexual relations with angelic beings. Additionally, there is no mention of homosexuality in these verses.

"Strange flesh"

The expression 'strange flesh' in the case of the angels describes their desire for human flesh. In the context of Sodom, this term is used in the exact same way, meaning a forbidden desire between an angel and a human, not a homosexual desire between two humans. In fact, from a hermeneutics standpoint, the term 'strange flesh' does not appear even once in the Scriptures in the context of homosexuality. Therefore, it should not be taken out of its usual meaning, nor should we infer that it refers to homosexuality without appropriate exegetical support.

Even logically, homosexuality cannot be considered 'strange flesh.' The term 'strange' does not fit homosexuality in itself because the act of homosexuality occurs within the boundaries of the same gender, race, and species, meaning the very same flesh. 'Strange' means something foreign or opposed to the flesh to which it is foreign. This eliminates the possibility of homosexuality.

The central sin in the story of Sodom and Gomorrah, which distinguishes these cities in their wickedness, was not idolatry or homosexuality. After all, many cities engaged in these acts, even to this day. The central sin in the story was the desire to engage with the angels who came to the city. If, in Genesis 6, the angels were the ones who initiated the forbidden sexual contact and yearned for strange human flesh, then here the roles are reversed, and it is the human who wickedly longs for the strange flesh, the flesh of the angel. For this reason, Sodom is mentioned twice in the New Testament in the context of angels, not homosexuality.

2 Peter 2:4-6 and Jude 6-7 describe angels punished for their transgressions, clarifying the identity of the "sons of God" in Genesis 6. These passages, which share textual and narrative similarities, explain how these angels left their assigned realm to engage in sexual relations with humans, resulting in their confinement in eternal darkness for judgment. Additionally, Sodom and Gomorrah are mentioned as examples. The coupling of these cities with the sinning angels suggests a similar transgression: the violation of divine boundaries, especially in sexual relations.

In 2 Peter 2:5, alongside the mention of the angels' sin, the flood of Noah is also referenced, indicating a connection between the two events. The proximity of these events in time, and more importantly, the implication that one event caused the other, strengthens the argument that the sin of the angels, which involved unnatural sexual relations with humans, had a direct impact on humanity, leading to "great wickedness" and the need for the great flood.

In summary, the sin of Sodom and Gomorrah, as depicted in 2 Peter 2:4-6 and Jude 6-7, may be interpreted as involving unnatural, forbidden relations with angelic beings, mirroring the earlier sin described in Genesis. It is noteworthy that neither Peter nor Jude specifically mention homosexuality in relation to the sin of Sodom.

---

1. John MacArthur, "What God Thinks of Homosexuals", Aug 21, 1977.

Leviticus 18:22

"It is an abomination"

> You shall not sleep with a male as one sleeps
> with a female; it is an abomination.
>
> Leviticus 18:22

C losely examining the Leviticus commandments reveals a mix of enduring moral principles and context-specific cultural rules. For instance, the condemnation of bestiality, incest, deceit, theft, and child sacrifice in Leviticus 18–20 aligns with universally acknowledged ethical standards upheld by most cultures today. Conversely, several other stipulations, such as prohibitions against shaving, wearing mixed fabrics, getting tattoos, removing fat from meat before eating it, planting diverse crops in the same field, and sexual relations during menstruation, are not emphasized in modern Christian doctrine. Some of these directives, like the prohibitions against shaving and getting tattoos, which were given in direct reference to idol worship, are largely accepted by most modern-day Christian denominations.

This raises questions about the applicability of these ancient mandates to modern Christians. For instance, the commandment against wearing mixed fabrics may seem culturally bound, as it is difficult to envision a contemporary Christian being condemned for wearing a cotton-polyester blend. Yet, the Old Testament does not explicitly categorize commandments into 'enduring moral principles' and 'context-specific cultural rules' categories.

The New Testament abrogates certain Old Testament laws, but it does not address the specific rule about mixed fabrics. This absence leaves room for interpretation and potential circular reasoning: a commandment is deemed 'cultural' because it is no longer practiced, and it is no longer practiced because it is considered 'cultural.'

This method proves inadequate for discerning the nature of the commandment prohibiting male same-sex relations. The lack of a clear-cut division between 'moral' and 'cultural' commandments complicates the task of determining the contemporary relevance of specific Old Testament laws.

Another approach might involve categorizing commandments based on their relation to sexual conduct, hypothesizing that all sex-related rules are moral imperatives. However, this theory is also flawed, as it does not address the overall ambiguity of non-sexual commandments and potentially misclassifies certain sexual commandments as cultural rather than moral.

An examination of the language used in these laws, specifically terms like "unclean" and "sin," does not yield a definitive distinction either, as these terms are sometimes used interchangeably, and neither is used in the context of male same-sex relations.

The term "abomination" is particularly noteworthy. It is used in the Old Testament to describe a range of offenses, including both cultural and seemingly moral transgressions. The Hebrew term for "abomination" associated with male same-sex relations differs from that used for forbidden foods and is often linked to idolatry-related offenses. This linguistic nuance opens the door to scholarly debate.

Some scholars argue that the relevant Leviticus passage condemns ritual cult prostitution associated with idolatry, which involves male same-sex sexual acts.

In Leviticus 18–20, God delivers a comprehensive set of instructions to Moses, intended to distinguish the Israelites from the polytheistic, pagan, idol-worshiping societies surrounding them. At the beginning of the chapter, God commands: *"You shall not do what is done in the land of Egypt where you lived, nor are you to do what is done in the land of Canaan where I am bringing you; you shall not walk in their statutes."* (Leviticus 18:3). These directives are meant to separate Israel from the pagan nations and consecrate the Israelites to God.

Leviticus 18:22 (and Leviticus 20:13) is also a directive meant to prevent Israel from worshiping idols, which often involved homosexual practices. For instance, during Sumerian times, a set of priests known as gala worked in Inanna's temples, where they performed elegies and lamentations. Some Sumerian proverbs seem to suggest that gala had a reputation for engaging in anal sex with men as part of their pagan rituals.[1] Likewise, several Akkadian proverbs seem to suggest that they also had homosexual proclivities as part of their idol-worshiping ceremonies.[2]

In addition, just one verse prior to *"You shall not sleep with a male as one sleeps with a female,"* verse 21 states, *"You shall not give any of your children to offer them to Molech,"* which also references an evil pagan idol-worshipping ritual. The idol-worshiping context helps us clarify why this act was forbidden.

Dennis Hollinger, the president of Gordon-Conwell Theological Seminary and Professor of Christian Ethics, explains:

> *The link between idolatry and sexual immorality is established by the frequent use of 'prostituting themselves' or 'adultery' to describe Hebrew idolatry [in the Old Testament]. Israel's unfaithfulness to God was not only a form of spiritual prostitution or adultery, but it also led to the physical acts themselves.*[3]

This interpretation is also acknowledged, albeit from a different perspective, by scholars who maintain a conservative view on homosexuality, such as Robert Gagnon, an associate professor of the New Testament at Pittsburgh Theological Seminary. Gagnon, a leading authority from the traditionalist camp, has extensively researched and critiqued homosexual practices from a biblical standpoint:

> I do not doubt that the circles out of which Leviticus 18:22 was produced had in view homosexual cult prostitution, at

least partly. Homosexual cult prostitution appears to have been the primary form in which homosexual intercourse was practiced in Israel.[4]

Scholars from various traditions concur that the biblical prohibitions against same-sex relations, particularly in Leviticus, likely relate to cult prostitution practices. This interpretation aligns with the broader objective of Leviticus: to distinguish the Israelites from neighboring polytheistic pagan cultures. This context is crucial in understanding the theological underpinnings of the laws presented in this passage. For instance, the prohibition against tattoos is not merely an objection to body ink; it addresses the Israelites' participation in known pagan rituals, a practice incompatible with their unique covenantal identity with God. The interdiction of tattoos, coupled with the ban on making cuts on the body or the head, illustrates the theological rationale underpinning these laws.

So, perhaps a practical approach to evaluating the relevance of a biblical commandment may involve examining its context, in our case, its relation to idol worship. For instance, an Old Testament verse that prohibits eating meat sacrificed to idols is found in Exodus 34:15: *"Be careful not to make a treaty with those who live in the land; for when they prostitute themselves to their gods and sacrifice to them, they will invite you and you will eat their sacrifices."* This verse warns against participating in the religious practices of idol worshippers, including consuming meat offered to their gods. However, in the New Testament, Paul offers a more nuanced view. In 1 Corinthians 8, Paul is addressing the issue of eating meat sacrificed to idols. There, he shifts towards permitting its consumption, assuming it's not eaten in honor of the gods. Similarly, one could argue that Leviticus 18:22, which addresses homosexuality in the context of idolatrous practices, suggests that in non-pagan contexts, some forms of homosexuality could be considered permissible.

If the condemnation of same-sex relations in Leviticus is rooted in its connection to idolatry and cult prostitution, this could rationalize both the severity of its punishment and its designation as an "abomination." Under this interpretation, such a condemnation would not necessarily extend to modern-day, consensual, and committed same-sex relationships. Conversely, if same-sex relations are condemned as inherently sinful across all contexts, then this prohibition would remain relevant today, including within committed relationships.

To resolve this ambiguity, it is insufficient to examine Leviticus in isolation. A comprehensive understanding necessitates considering these Old Testament laws in the light of New Testament teachings, just as we did with Genesis 19. The New Testament provides a recontextualization of Old Testament laws, offering insights into which aspects of the Mosaic Law were culturally specific and which moral principles are universally applicable. This approach requires thoroughly examining the New Testament's treatment of issues such as idolatry, sexual morality, and the nature of Christian freedom under the new covenant established by Christ. This holistic approach enables a more nuanced and theologically informed interpretation of Levitical laws and their relevance to contemporary Christian ethics.

---

1. Leick, Gwendolyn (2013). Sex and Eroticism in Mesopotamian Literature.

2. Murray, Stephen O (1997). Islamic homosexualities: culture, history, and literature. NYU Press.

3. Dennis P. Hollinger, The Meaning of Sex: Christian Ethics and the Moral Life, page 64.

4. Robert A. J. Gagnon, The Bible and Homosexual Practice: Texts and Hermeneutics (Nashville: Abingdon Press, 2001) 130.

1 Corinthians 6:9–11

"Arsenokoitai will not inherit the kingdom of God"

⁹ Or do you not know that the unrighteous will not inherit the kingdom of God? Do not be deceived; neither the sexually immoral, nor idolaters, nor adulterers, nor *arsenokoitai*, ¹⁰ nor thieves, nor the greedy, nor those habitually drunk, nor verbal abusers, nor swindlers, will inherit the kingdom of God. ¹¹ Such were some of you; but you were washed, but you were sanctified, but you were justified in the name of the Lord Jesus Christ and in the Spirit of our God.

1 Corinthians 6:9–11

The Greek term "arsenokoitai" is translated in various ways across different Bible versions. While some translations interpret it as "homosexuals," others, like the

American Standard Version, the English Revised Version, and the King James Version, employ phrases with broader meanings, such as "abusers of themselves with mankind" in the KJV.

The term "arsenokoitai" appears only twice in the Bible, in 1 Corinthians 6:9 and also in 1 Timothy 1:10:

> For the sexually immoral, *arsenokoitai*, slave traders, liars, perjurers, and whatever else is contrary to sound teaching
>
> 1 Timothy 1:10

In 1 Timothy 1:10, the term is included in a list of behaviors that are contrary to sound teaching. The KJV translation of this verse uses the phrase *"for them that defile themselves with mankind,"* instead of directly referencing homosexuality as some other translations do.

Some scholars argue that "arsenokoitai" specifically refers to men who engage in same-sex relations, hence the translation to "homosexuals" in some modern versions. Others suggest that the term could be referring to idol-worshipping-related homosexual acts, not necessarily to homosexual behavior in general. "Arsenokoitai" is a compound Greek word derived from "arsen," meaning "male," and "koite," meaning "bed." This combination appears in the Greek translation of the Leviticus passage, leading some scholars to suggest that Paul might have created this term specifically in reference to that text.

Its exact meaning in the context of the New Testament writings, however, is not universally agreed upon. The ambiguity arises from its rare usage in ancient texts, leading to various interpretations in modern translations.

The question arises: was Paul's use of "arsenokoitai" an allusion to Leviticus? If so, was his intention to address the cult prostitution mentioned in Leviticus 18 and Romans 1, or was he making a broader condemnation of male-male sexual relations?

Scholars also debate about interpreting "arsenokoitai" in conjunction with "malakoi," another Greek term. In the New International Version (NIV), "malakoi" is translated as "male prostitutes," while in the KJV, it is rendered as "effeminate." This juxtaposition in translations raises further questions about the specific behaviors or characteristics Paul addressed in his epistles.

For example, the 1990 edition of the Catholic Study Bible, which is ultra-conservative in nature and not at all aligned with pro-gay interpretations, suggested a pagan ritual context:

The Greek word translated as "*boy prostitutes*" [malakoi] designated catamites, i.e., boys or young men who were kept for purposes of prostitution, a practice not uncommon in the Greco-Roman world. In Greek mythology this was the function of Ganymede, the "*cupbearer of the gods*," whose Latin name was Catamitus. The term translated "*practicing homosexuals*" [arsenokoitai] refers to adult males who indulged in homosexual practices with such boys.

The cultural context of Greek society during Paul's time, where married men engaging in sexual relations with boys was prevalent, presents a complex backdrop for interpreting biblical texts. This practice, widely accepted in ancient Greek culture, is undoubtedly condemned in contemporary society for various ethical reasons. However, understanding this historical practice in its pagan context is crucial in discerning whether Paul's references to same-sex relations were addressing such specific instances or making a broader moral statement about homosexuality, including consensual and committed adult relationships.

The translation of key Greek terms in the New Testament further complicates this interpretation. For example, the New International Version initially translated certain words as "*male prostitutes*" but later revised this in 2011 to "*men who have sex with men.*" This shift in translation reflects the ongoing debate about the exact nature of the behaviors Paul was condemning, with the former option clearly referring to the pagan practice of idol worship. Was Paul specifically targeting pagan practices within his cultural context, such as pederasty or idolatrous sexual rituals? Or was his condemnation intended to be universally applied to all forms of homosexual activity?

The NIV's translation, which was made by an ultra-conservative committee, exemplifies the challenges in understanding ancient texts within their historical context and translating them accurately for a modern audience.

On the other hand, other Bible translations have done the exact opposite by recognizing that the text does not speak of homosexuality in general and have updated the text accordingly:

> Do you not know that wrongdoers will not inherit the kingdom of God? Do not be deceived! The sexually immoral,

idolaters, adulterers, *male prostitutes, men who engage in illicit sex*, [10] thieves, the greedy, drunkards, revilers, swindlers—none of these will inherit the kingdom of God.

1 Corinthians 6:9-10 (NRSVUE)

Another relevant example is the biblical injunction against usury, or the charging of interest on loans, which is addressed in several Old Testament passages (e.g., Exodus 22:25, Leviticus 25:36-37, Deuteronomy 23:19-20). In these contexts, usury was seen as exploitative, especially when it involved lending to the poor or fellow Israelites in need.

However, in contemporary society, the charging of interest is a standard and accepted practice in banking and finance and a crucial part of any thriving economy. This shift in perception is not due to a change in the moral stance on lending money with interest but the understanding that it may, under some circumstances, cause exploitation. The existence of usury is evidence of an evolution in economic systems and societal norms. In modern economies, interest is seen as a necessary component of financial transactions and not inherently exploitative in the way it was in the agrarian societies of ancient Israel.

The last example to illustrate the importance of contextual understanding in biblical interpretation is the dietary laws in the Old Testament. In Leviticus, there are specific prohibitions against consuming certain foods, such as pork and shellfish (Leviticus 11). These dietary restrictions, which also had to do with separating Israel from the pagan nations, were integral to the Hebrew culture and religious practices of the time.

However, in the New Testament, particularly in the book of Acts, Peter has a vision where he is shown various unclean animals and is told, "*What God has made clean, do not call common*" (Acts 10:15). This vision and subsequent teachings in the New Testament, have been understood by many Christians to mean that the Old Testament dietary laws are no longer binding for Christians. This shift reflects a broader theological understanding that with the advent of the New Covenant through Christ, many Old Testament laws were fulfilled and transformed or should only be applied to specific contexts.

Just as the biblical injunctions against usury were a response to the economic practices and potential for exploitation in ancient times and just as the dietary laws in the Old Testament were context-specific, applying to a particular cultural and religious setting, and were reinterpreted in the New Testament, so too might the references to same-sex practices in Paul's letters be contextually bound with the understanding they refer to the practice of idol-worship.

Furthermore, the comparison with tax collectors in the New Testament is also apt; just as negative references to tax collectors in Jesus' time are understood within the framework of their corrupt practices, rather than a blanket condemnation of all tax collectors throughout history, so too might the references to homosexuals be contextually bound.

When examining passages like 1 Corinthians 6:9, the key lies in the interpretation of "arsenokoitai" and "malakoi." If these terms refer specifically to practices like pederasty or idolatrous rituals, then the Bible may not directly address the morality of committed, consensual same-sex relationships. However, if "arsenokoitai" is interpreted as a blanket condemnation of all homosexual acts, this interpretation would have broader implications for understanding other passages in Leviticus and Romans.

This ambiguity leads to a theological dilemma. Making a definitive argument in either direction is challenging, and the risk of either endorsing what could be sinful behavior or unjustly condemning morally acceptable relationships is significant. Each interpretation appears sound, yet neither is entirely convincing, leaving a gap in clarity and certainty. Ultimately, this issue highlights the complexity of biblical interpretation, especially when contemporary understandings of sexuality and relationships intersect with ancient texts, cultural norms, and practices such as idolatry.

However, in this gap of understanding lies the opportunity to extend grace and empathy, allowing room for more than one opinion alone to be voiced.

Romans 1:18-32

"Males with males committing shameful acts"

18 For the wrath of God is revealed from heaven against all ungodliness and unrighteousness of people who suppress the truth in unrighteousness, **19** because that which is known about God is evident within them; for God made it evident to them. **20** For since the creation of the world His invisible *attributes, that is*, His eternal power and divine nature, have been clearly perceived, being understood by what has been made, so that they are without excuse. **21** For even though they knew God, they did not honor Him as God or give thanks, but they became futile in their reasonings, and their senseless hearts were darkened. **22** Claiming to be wise, they became fools, **23** and they exchanged the glory of the incorruptible God for an image in the form of corruptible mankind, of birds, four-footed animals, and crawling creatures.

24 Therefore God gave them up to vile impurity in the lusts of their hearts, so that their bodies would be dishonored among them. 25 For they exchanged the truth of God for falsehood, and worshiped and served the creature rather than the Creator, who is blessed forever. Amen.

26 For this reason God gave them over to degrading passions; for their women exchanged natural relations for that which is contrary to nature, 27 and likewise the men, too, abandoned natural relations with women and burned in their desire toward one another, males with males committing shameful acts and receiving in their own persons the due penalty of their error.

28 And just as they did not see fit to acknowledge God, God gave them up to a depraved mind, to do those things that are not proper, 29 *people* having been filled with all unrighteousness, wickedness,

greed, *and* evil; full of envy, murder, strife, d e c e i t , *a n d* m a l i c e ; *t h e y are* gossips, [30] slanderers, haters of God, insolent, arrogant, boastful, inventors of evil, disobedient to parents, [31] without u n d e r s t a n d i n g , untrustworthy, unfeeling, *and* unmerciful; [32] and although they know the ordinance of God, that those who practice such things are worthy of death, they not only do the same, but also approve of those who practice them.

Romans 1:18-32

I n ancient Roman society, sexual behaviors and preferences were not categorized in the same way as in modern Western societies. The Romans did not primarily think in terms of "homosexual" and "heterosexual," and there were no Latin words for these concepts.[1] Instead, their focus was more on the roles of dominance and submission in sexual relations.

Kelly J. Murphy, a philosophy and religion professor at Central Michigan University, says:

We have to remember that Paul and the world Paul lived in did not understand gender the same way that we do today, and also that Paul is using that example to lead up to his argument against worshipping idols. Opinions are split about whether Paul is upset about heterosexual people having same-sex relations or about pederasty -- but the larger point is that worshipping idols instead of God leads to mistakes in morality.

The morality of a Roman man's sexual behavior was largely determined by his social standing and the status of his sexual partner rather than the gender of the partner. It was socially acceptable for a freeborn Roman man to have sexual relations with both women and young men, particularly if the young men were of a lower status. The key was that a man maintained his role as the dominant, penetrative partner, which was aligned with Roman ideals of masculinity and self-discipline.

In Romans 1-3, Paul argues that all people—Jewish and Gentile— are in need of salvation. In Romans 2, he speaks to his fellow Jews, saying that even one violation of the Law renders them in need of reconciliation to God.

In Romans 1:18-32, Paul discusses pagans who have strayed from God, choosing idol worship over honoring Him. This idolatry, according to Paul, led God to allow these individuals to engage in sexual immorality, seemingly abandoning what is described as "natural" sexual relations for "shameless acts" with one another. This passage concludes with a list of various sins associated with these idolaters.

A critical examination of this text raises complex questions about the nature of sexual sin and its association with idolatry. One interpretation suggests that the shift to homosexuality is depicted as a consequence of idol worship. This raises the question: Does the passage imply that heterosexual individuals became homosexual as a result of straying from God, and is homosexuality thereby a divine punishment? This interpretation hardly makes any sense.

Paul presents a sequence of arguments that follow a specific, non-reversible order. He starts by addressing the turning away from God and the subsequent idol worship. Following this, he describes how these individuals engage in harmful sexual practices linked to their idolatry. The progression in Paul's argument is deliberate and cannot be simply inverted.

Therefore, it would be erroneous to conclude that an individual's homosexuality is a direct indication of having turned away from God.

The structure of Paul's argument here is crucial: the departure from God leads to idolatry, which then leads to various forms of sexual immorality. This specific order of events is foundational to Paul's message in Romans 1 and illustrates the theological and moral decline he attributes to idol worship. The argument is not just about the actions themselves but about the underlying cause-and-effect relationship between idolatry and subsequent immoral behaviors.

Further inquiry into the text reveals that sinful sexual behavior, including some forms of homosexual acts, is directly linked to the act of idolatry. This connection is emphasized twice in the passage, suggesting a strong correlation between idol worship and the subsequent sexual immorality. This specific coupling of idolatry with sexual sin, particularly homosexual acts, demands a deeper understanding of the cultural and religious context of Paul's time. A. J. Droge explains:

> In its attitude toward Greek religion the NT adopts a tradition going back to Hellenistic Judaism (Wisdom of Solomon 13–15). This tradition finds its clearest expression in Rom 1:18–32, where Paul criticizes pagan religion (Castellino 1963: 255–63). According to

him, the history of Greek religion is one of degradation and corruption spurred on by men who have suppressed the truth.[2]

Likewise, in the conservative "Word Biblical Commentary: Romans 1-8," James Dunn notes that Paul's critique *"is a characteristic expression of Jewish antipathy toward the practice of homosexuality so prevalent in the Greco-Roman world."*

Certain idol-worshipping cults of the period incorporated sexual practices, including some forms of homosexual acts, into their rituals. These practices, ranging from cult temple prostitution to castration and same-sex rites, were in the context of the worship of various deities. Understanding this context clarifies why Paul connects idolatry so closely with sexual immorality, including homosexual behavior, in his letter to the Romans.

Sexuality, in itself, is not inherently sinful; rather, it is the context and manner in which it is expressed that can render it problematic. For instance, certain sexual acts deemed acceptable within the confines of a committed marital relationship might be viewed negatively in different contexts, such as those lacking consent or involving incestuous relationships. This perspective suggests that Paul's discourse in Romans 1 might not be a blanket condemnation of homosexuality. Instead, it could be addressing the misuse or inappropriate expression of sexual behavior rather than the orientation itself. This interpretation aligns with the broader biblical principle that the morality of sexual acts is largely determined by their context—especially in relation to idol worship— and the nature of the relationships in which they occur.

Paul's use of terms like "natural," "unnatural," and "shameful" in describing same-sex relations does not necessarily imply that all such relationships are sinful. In 1 Corinthians 11:13-14, he similarly labels long hair on men as "unnatural," yet this is widely interpreted as reflecting first-century customs rather than a universal Christian rule. The Bible itself shows that long hair in men, as in the Nazirite vow (Numbers 6:5), can be honorable. Samson's decision to cut his hair was shameful in his context, while his long hair was actually a source of strength (Judges 16:17-19). What is honorable and shameful varies across times, cultures, and contexts.

Therefore, Paul's references to "shameful lusts" (1:26) and "inflamed with lust" (1:27) in Romans may specifically target the pagan culture's degrading forms of homosexuality prevalent in his time, like pagan temple prostitution.

Paul's rhetorical strategy in Romans is analogous to the approach used by the prophet Nathan with King David in 2 Samuel 12. Nathan used a parable to lead David to self-condemnation, and similarly, Paul leads his audience through a narrative designed to highlight their own culpability in sin. By initially focusing on the sinful acts of idol worshippers, Paul engages his audience's agreement on the wrongness of these acts. However, he then shifts the focus, pointing out that all are sinners in need of redemption, effectively illustrating the universality of sin and the need for salvation.

The crux of Paul's message in Romans 1:18-32 is not solely to condemn the sexual immorality associated with idol worship but to use it as a vivid illustration of the broader theme of human sinfulness and the need for grace. This interpretation suggests that the passage's primary focus is not the inherent sinfulness of homosexuality but the broader context of idolatry and its corrupting influence.

While this analysis offers insights into the cultural and religious backdrop of Paul's epistle, it does not provide clear directives regarding modern-day committed gay relationships. The passage's characterization of certain sexual acts as "shameful" and "unnatural" complicates the interpretation, particularly when viewed through the lens of contemporary understandings of sexual orientation and ethics.

Paul elucidates that the Gentiles, although not recipients of the Law of Moses, are still culpable for turning away from God. This culpability is underscored in verse 20, emphasizing that God has revealed Himself to them, yet they chose idol worship over acknowledging Him. Consequently, God permitted them to follow the lust of their hearts in following idols, leading to various forms of sexual immorality.

Paul's discussion of these sexual behaviors is not an exploration of sexual orientation as understood in contemporary terms. Instead, he focuses on the acts themselves as a departure from what he describes as "natural" relations. This interpretation implies that it is not the orientation that is condemned but the actions driven by unrestrained lust concerning idol worship.

Paul's argument suggests that heterosexual individuals engaged in homosexual acts as a form of idolatrous worship. This interpretation aligns with the historical context of Roman society, where sexual practices were often intertwined with pagan rituals. In this view, the "unnatural" acts Paul describes are not about committed, loving relationships but are aimed at lust-driven behaviors such as orgies, castration, and male-male degrading prostitution in pagan temples.

In conclusion, Romans 1 can be seen as focusing on the broader theme of idolatry and its corrupting influence on human behavior. The passage underscores the destructive nature and consequences in the life of those who worship idols and the need for salvation, which transcends specific sexual practices. It is a call to recognize the pervasiveness of sin and the need for redemption rather than a specific commentary on homosexuality or the nature of committed same-sex relationships.

---

1. Craig Williams, Roman Homosexuality (Oxford University Press, 1999, 2010), p. 304, citing Saara Lilja, Homosexuality in Republican and Augustan Rome (Societas Scientiarum Fennica, 1983), p. 122.

2. A. J. Droge, "Apologetics, NT," ed. David Noel Freedman, The Anchor Yale Bible Dictionary (New York: Doubleday, 1992), 303.

Conclusion

The prevailing perception that the Bible is staunchly anti-gay perpetuates a deep-seated conflict between the gay community and many Christian congregations. This dichotomy has led to an ongoing struggle marked by misunderstanding and hostility on both sides and, at times, sadly, included violence.

This has cornered many individuals into a false dilemma: feeling compelled to choose between adherence to what they believe is biblical teachings and expressing love and acceptance toward their gay friends and family members. This perceived mutual exclusivity has significant implications for both personal faith and inter-community relations.

A more nuanced examination of biblical texts is essential to address this issue. The interpretation of scriptures related to homosexuality often lacks a thorough consideration of historical, cultural, and context. Simplistic readings of these texts can lead to broad generalizations and misinterpretations. For instance, the translation and interpretation of terms like "arsenokoitai" in the New Testament have varied significantly among different Bible versions, reflecting the complexity and subjectivity inherent in translating ancient texts.

To bridge the gap between the homosexual community and the church, a more empathetic and informed approach to scripture is needed. This includes acknowledging the historical and cultural distance between the biblical texts and the present day and considering how the Bible's overarching themes of love, justice, and mercy can inform contemporary understandings of ancient religious texts.

Such an approach could help mitigate the conflict by offering a perspective of the Bible that is neither inherently anti-gay nor dismissive of biblical authority. It could pave the way for a more inclusive and compassionate dialogue, where individuals do not feel forced to choose between their faith and loving their homosexual friends.

If one insists on viewing homosexuality as sinful, it is important to bear in mind two key points:

First, is that the same biblical passages that some interpret as condemning homosexuality place it in the same list or category as sins like gossip and greed.

This contextualization suggests a need for a balanced perspective on the nature and impact of different sins. It raises the question of why certain sins, such as gossip and greed, which are equally listed, do not receive the same level of attention or condemnation.

Secondly, homosexual individuals in committed relationships do not cause harm to others, in contrast to behaviors like gossip, theft, or lying, which have direct negative impacts on individuals and communities. Despite this, there is a noticeable lack of focus in many Christian circles on addressing sins that actively harm others while eagerly attacking the homosexual community. The emphasis often appears disproportionately placed on condemning individuals in homosexual relationships.

At the same time, sins that cause tangible harm, such as gossip, receive little attention in church sermons, books, and articles, or public protests. This discrepancy calls for reevaluating the priorities and focus in the Church's teaching and activism.

Afterword

As we conclude this book, it's important to recognize that theological discourse, by its very nature, often presents complex and multifaceted issues that may not yield definitive answers. In our journey through these pages, we have explored diverse perspectives and interpretations, each offering its own insights and understanding. It is essential to acknowledge that it is perfectly acceptable, and even necessary, to agree to disagree on certain theological matters. The realm of theology, steeped in centuries of scholarship and debate, cannot always provide absolute certainty in every aspect. This acknowledgment is not a sign of weakness but rather an expression of humility and intellectual honesty. It serves as a reminder that our understanding is continually evolving and that there is always more to learn and consider.

Embracing this perspective should encourage us to remain humble in our convictions, compassionate in our interactions, and open to the views of others. In a world teeming with diverse beliefs and opinions, engaging respectfully with those who think differently is not just a virtue but a necessity. It fosters a culture of dialogue and mutual respect, where differing viewpoints are tolerated and welcomed as opportunities for growth and deeper understanding. As we close this book, let us carry forward the spirit of open-mindedness and empathy, recognizing that our collective pursuit of theological understanding is enriched, not diminished, by the diversity of thoughts and beliefs that each of us brings to the table.

***

Before concluding this book (or powering down your e-reader), I would like to request a small favor. Having devoted considerable time and effort to crafting this concise and accessible book, your feedback would be immensely valuable. It would be greatly appreciated if you could take a moment to rate it on Amazon. Your rating or review is an excellent way to show your support and acknowledge the extensive research and effort that went into distilling this complex topic into an easily digestible format. Thank you very much for your time and consideration.

Please check out my other books at:
www.eitan.bar/books

Printed in Great Britain
by Amazon